Mabel's Mask

Written by Sarah Greenwell,
Illustrated by Jonathan Hart

This book belongs to:

....

Mabel's Mask

*To Lincoln, Eve and Arbor. You are brave, you are
strong, and you make Mom so happy.*
SG

*To all the children who grew up without seeing
themselves represented, you are loved.*
JH

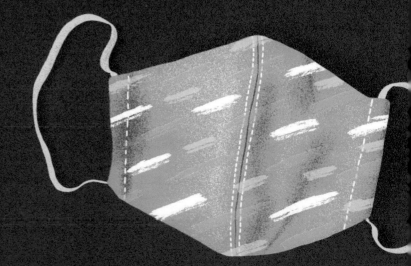

Mabel's mask has come
from Mars!

(Or somewhere else
that's very far.)

She puts it on and runs inside

To show it to her Aunt with pride.

David's daddies
made his mask.

David helped them
with the task.

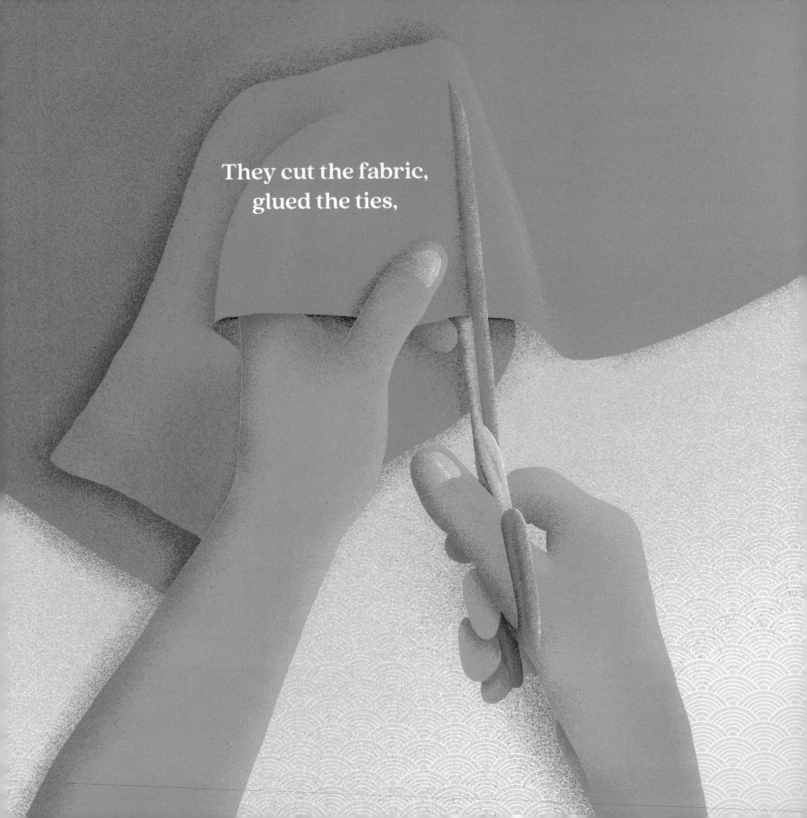

Then tied it to the
perfect size.

Tia's tie-dye mask is cool!

She'll wear it when she goes to school.

She'll show her friends
the swirls of blue,

*The purple, red
and yellow, too.*

Stevie's sad about his mask.

"What's going on?" Daddy asks.

He misses play without one on.

"*Just until the sickness is gone.*"

Grace is going to the store.
It is different than before.

She puts on her mask,
holds Gram's hand,

Then waves "Hi!" to
the grocery man.

Mae's mom wears her mask at night.
Before work, tucks her in tight.

Mae says, "Mom, I wear a mask, too.
So I'm a hero, just like you!"